It's Been Too Long!!!
Lessons Learned From Traffic Jams

DarLisa L. Meaders

Copyright © 2016 DarLisa L. Meaders

All rights reserved.

ISBN-13:978-1-943342-02-0

DEDICATION

This book is dedicated to my family, and friends. To my parents, Darrin & Lisa Meaders, thank you for naming me DarLisa; which means Bold and Devoted to God. You have shaped the woman I have become; I appreciate your love, support and guidance over the year. To my siblings thank you for putting up with your "sista mama". I should've used the time I spent in the house (instead of playing outside with you guys) to write books; at least the Lord is restoring that time. I love each of you and pray that the Lord blesses your ministries: D.D. building things, DarLa-singing, and DarLynn-gymnastics.

To my Auntie Win-Win, thank you for knowing the right words to say, inspiring me to accomplish my goals and dreams, and allowing me to be your daughter. To my granny, who is the best grandma ever; thank you for helping me edit this book and providing me with wisdom & insight on serving God. To my entire family near and far, related and not related, I love you! To my friends, I know we don't talk much, but I pray for you often. Paw-Paw would say "Everything is in Divine Order" and "All God Wants for Me Is Something Good". I still believe that.

DarLisa L. Meaders

CONTENTS

	Acknowledgments	I
	Introduction	1
1	What Time Is It?	Pg 2
2	It's Too Early	Pg 5
3	It's Right On Time	Pg 7
4	It's Been Too Long	Pg 10
5	It's About Time	Pg 13
6	Time Will Tell	Pg 17
	Words For The Road	Pg 19
	Questions For Your Journey	Pg 23
	Prayer For Traffic Jams	Pg 27
	Helpful Resources	Pg 28
	About The Author	Pg 31

ACKNOWLEDGMENTS

I would like to express my gratitude to the Almighty God who provided me with revelations during traffic jams. To Emma Meaders, Elicia Sashington, and Donna Jackson; thank you from the bottom of my heart for helping me during the editing process. I would like to also thank Marcie Hill who I consider to be my author accountability partner. Thanks are also due to the Destined To Publish Authors Conference hosted by Heavenly Enterprises. The conference provided me with inspiration and tools to continue on this journey to publishing It's Been Too Long! I can't forget all those people who directly and indirectly contributed to this work.
Thank you all!

INTRODUCTION

I know I'm not the only person who has felt like "It's been too long!" When we have our life planned out on a time frame for certain events and experiences (such as graduation, marriage, children, etc.) we actually limit God's ability to lead and guide us according to His perfect plan. It is easy to become impatient, anxious, and even frustrated when we feel like our lives aren't going the way we want them to. But I was reminded that God's timing is the best timing.

I tried reading books about the importance of patience and waiting on God's timing but they were too long. As I drove to work in the mornings my commute became a blessing. I would spend the time in a seemingly frustrating situation (traffic) praising the Lord, listening to encouraging music, and learning lessons from traffic jams. I began to feel a sense of peace and gratitude as I recalled events, experiences and circumstances that developed and shaped me into who I am.

The Word of God comes in many forms; in this book the Message Bible (MSG) is used to help illustrate the words of the Bible. I don't encourage anyone to read this while in a literal traffic jam but do read it when it seems like you are experiencing a traffic jam in your life. I hope this book blesses you and that you pass it along. I pray that you will learn your own lessons in traffic jams.

1
WHAT TIME IS IT?

The first few hours being awake can be a vulnerable time. It can determine your mood and dictate your response for the rest of the day. What time do you wake up? What time do you eat breakfast? What time do you get to work? What time do you eat lunch? What time do you leave work? What time do you run your errands? What time do you get home? What time do you eat dinner? What time does your favorite T.V. show come on? What time do you take a shower? What time do you go to bed? What time do you wake up to start it all over again?

As you read that paragraph, I'm sure you asked what time will these questions end? Many times in our life we are so concerned with our daily routine and common problems that we forget the most important questions. What time are we spending with God? How long did we spend praying or listening quietly for His response? How long did we spend praising him for waking us up, or getting us to our workplace safely? How often do we acknowledge the many other blessing he provides us daily? Sometimes we get so concerned with the issues of life we overlook that we are living.

When I was first learning to drive as a teenager, I took my father's driving tips the wrong way. I would become withdrawn and begin crying when he gave me constructive criticism on my driving skills. Back then, I thought he was being harsh, but over time, I realized that he knew how much responsibility comes with being a driver. My dad loved me and wanted to make sure that I was prepared and ready for the task ahead.

I can remember one instance in particular, my senior year in high school, when I was driving my sister and cousin to choir practice. We were running late, so I moved over to the third lane. Since I was a beginning driver my dad insisted that I "stay out of the third lane" but that day I chose to go against his suggestion. While in traffic, in the third lane, going approximately 25 miles per hour the vehicle in front of me slowed down to 0. I frantically attempted to move back into the second lane but tapped the right side bumper of the car in front of me.

Fortunately, everyone involved was fine and there was minimal damage to the vehicles. I thought he was being ridiculous and cruel by telling me to stay out of the third lane but he was just warning me and trying to protect me from situations like this. I got a ticket for following too close and a lecture from my dad. I can't remember the whole conversation that evening, but I remember him saying "I told you to stay out the third lane." It wasn't in a condescending or cruel attitude, it was in a tone that let me know his true intent for the instructions he gave me.

Sometimes you may not be ready for certain speeds or situations and there is nothing wrong with being in the first and second lane. I felt worried and anxious about getting to my destination on time but neglected to realize that getting there safely was more important. If I had been less worried about getting to where I was going so fast, I may have avoided that situation.

When I find myself questioning God's timing and saying "it's been too long!" I will read Philippians 4:6-7 in the Message Bible. "Don't fret or worry. Instead of worrying, pray. Let petitions and praises shape your worries into prayers, letting God know your concerns. Before you know it, a sense of God's wholeness, everything coming together for good, will come and settle you down. It's wonderful what happens when Christ displaces worry at the center of your life."

Don't be preoccupied with what time it is. While you are looking at the clock, you may be missing an opportunity to grow and learn from your circumstances. Be patient because traffic jams are only temporary. Traffic jams may be annoying, irritating, distracting, and frustrating, (the list goes on and on),. but you can't let them dictate your emotions, reactions, or impact your future.

Words for the Road

No matter which method of transportation we use, God covers us and controls our speed and timing.

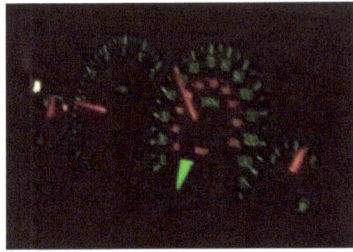

2
IT'S TOO EARLY

Sometimes you get to your destination and realize you have time to spare. You thought with the traffic, possible trains, buses, slower cars, and pedestrians, it should have taken you longer to get to your destination. Instead of spending that extra time complaining about being too early, spend that time with the one who got you to your destination safely.

One day I woke up at 4:00am to the sound of my phone alarm. I don't remember why the alarm was set for that time. After ignoring the alarm a few times, I turned the alarm off frantically and went back to bed. I still had a few hours before I had to get ready for work.

I was awakened by my phone's alarm at 6:00am. My body was still tired so I laid my head back down for a few extra minutes. By the time I looked up it was almost 6:30am. I finally got out the bed and got ready to go to work. I didn't leave the house until almost 7:10am which is a lot later than when I usually leave. As I walked out the door, I noticed that there were no children on their way to school and the crossing guard's car wasn't parked down the street.

I blamed it on report-card pick up and continued towards my car. I started the car, turned on Pandora and began my morning commute. While turning the corner, I noticed the clock on my dashboard which read 6:16 am. In my rush to turn off the phone alarm, I somehow changed the time zone on my phone. I was up and out early that morning. Instead of being frustrated by leaving the house earlier, I used that extra time to be more productive.

Being more productive involves taking steps to accomplish your goals. They can be short term goals like taking a few extra steps a day or balancing your check book more often {insert a few of your own). Long term goals may include paying off a credit card or student loan, or writing that book {insert a few of your own}. When we think that things are happening too soon we must remember that "Everything Is In Divine Order."

Words for the Road

Turn an early arrival into an opportunity for productivity.

3
IT'S RIGHT ON TIME

Have you ever overslept and knew you wouldn't make it to where you needed to be on time? One day I thought I was going to be late and almost decided to stay home, but I arrived right on time. I would have missed out on whatever opportunity awaited me at my destination because I gave up and quit. I won't let changes in timing effect my optimistic outlook on life.

In 2012, I began pursing my Master's Degree in Public Health from the University of Illinois at Chicago. The first semester I worked part-time and went to school full time. My second semester I had the opportunity to work at a high school as a teacher's assistant. I went in for several interviews and was offered and accepted a full time position.

Since I can do all things through Christ (Philippians 4:13 NKJV) who strengthens me, I accepted the challenge. I worked from 8:00 am until 4:00 pm and went to class throughout the week. Somehow I managed my time between work, school, family and my relationship although it wasn't an easy task. I decided to spread my course load out and take a few extra electives to ensure my successful completion of the program. This decision pushed my graduation date to May of 2014. I felt like I had done something wrong, and was disappointed in myself. A two year master's program took me three years. The Lord spoke to me about my misinterpretation of His plan.

Shortly, after deciding to continue graduate school for another year, I found out that my brother would be graduating with a Bachelor's from North Carolina A&T State University in May of 2014. His graduation would have been on the same exact day in as my initial graduation day. My family would have had to make some tough decisions about whose graduation they would attend. I would have insisted that everyone go to my brother's graduation since I had already graduated with a Bachelor's Degree. It's a wonderful feeling to have people recognize you for accomplishing your goals.

In retrospect, although I would have wanted everyone to support my brother, I would have felt frustrated and upset about my decision later. I didn't' realize God's plan at the time, but He was working it out for our good. It's never too late to finish something you started or even start something you want to finish. I work with youth who may have been out of school for a while or are a little older than their peers. Sometimes I hear them discouraging themselves or talking about how they should have graduated a long time ago.

I interject myself into their conversations and remind them that they are making progress and it's never too late to achieve a goal, or make a change for the better. Although they may not always listen to my advice, I pray that the seeds of positivity that I plant everyday will sprout up, and the students will plant more positive seeds in other people.

Words for the Road

Detours can seem devastating but remember God has a plan that goes farther than we can see.

4
IT'S BEEN TOO LONG!

Have you ever thought that you were out of place or that things (school, marriage, children, job search etc.) were taking too long? As I sat in traffic on my way to work, I tried to change lanes but a lady in a white car wouldn't let me over. I was frustrated because I like to change lanes systematically. This lady was messing with my morning driving routine. If I know a merge of highways is coming up or I need to get off at the next exit, I want to be prepared. As I turned to give her a funny look, a song came blaring through the car speakers: "*Let Go & Let God*" by Dwayne Woods. At that moment I stopped trying to annoy the other driver and focused on myself.

A few minutes later the same lady in the white car who wouldn't let me over was behind me. As I looked at her position, I realized that the flow of traffic changes frequently. It can be slow one minute and fast the next. The flow of traffic doesn't matter as long as you get to your destination safely. I began praising God because he gave me another lesson from a traffic jam.

When I was younger I performed in oratory competitions, reciting poems and sharing my gift with others. Somewhere down the line I neglected my gift. Recently, I started using my gift reciting a poem entitled "I'm Determined To Be Somebody Someday" by Dr. William Herbert Brewster. Within a month I recited the poem in front of high school and grammar school students, as well as the New Faith Toastmaster's International Club. I also competed in a speech competition in which I won 3rd place. I have a renewed passion for public speaking. Imagine if I would have convinced myself not to try because it had been "too long".

Isaiah 40:27-31 (MSG) talks about letting go. "Why would you ever complain O Jacob (insert your name here), or whine, Israel saying "God has lost track of me He doesn't care what happens to me"? Don't you know anything? Haven't you been listening? God doesn't come and go. God lasts. He's the creator of all you can see or imagine. He doesn't get tired out, doesn't pause to catch his breath. And he knows everything inside and out. He energizes those who get tired out, gives fresh strength to dropouts. For even young people tire and drop out, young folk in their prime stumble and fall. But those who wait upon God get fresh strength. They spread their wings and soar like eagles. They run and don't get tired, they walk and don't lag behind."

Don't lose hope because it's been too long. Your circumstances can be discouraging, disappointing and frustrating {insert the emotion you are feeling during your circumstances} when you seem to be off course. Detours don't last forever. God motivates us to do better. He gives us the strength to take new opportunities, go back to school, share our testimonies, write books, speak or sing in front of crowds, do gymnastics, inspire others, bowl 300 games, build and engineer new technology, {insert your gift/talent here}. Whatever you have been holding off, do it! It's time! He will give you the strength and resources to do it.

Words for the Road

Don't get frustrated with the position of other drivers. God has you right where he wants you to be.

5
IT'S ABOUT TIME

My husband and I began dating his last semester of college. We went on a bowling date which included two of my siblings, then talked on the phone for hours and the rest is history. When he graduated, I was excited for him but disappointed because our love story had just began. He would be back in Chicago, IL and I would be near Grand Rapids, MI almost 170 miles away. Being in a long distance relationship for the next two years was a trying time for us.

I used to wish that he stayed in Grand Rapids. But I have come to the realization that everything turned out the way it should be. I can only imagine how our lives would be different today if he would have moved to be closer to me. Would I have focused enough to complete my bachelor's degree? Would I have continued to pursue my graduate degree in public health? Would he have explored his interest in becoming a teacher? Would he have gone to graduate school? I don't know, but I'm grateful that God didn't let me have my own way because He knows what's best for me.

Isaiah 55:8-11 MSG, says "I don't think the way you think. The way you work isn't the way I work." GOD's decree, "For as the sky soars high above earth, so the way I work surpasses the way you work, and the way I think is beyond the way you think. Just as rain and snow descend from the skies and don't go back until they've watered the earth, Doing their work of making things grow and blossom, producing seed for farmers and food for the hungry, So will the words that come out of my mouth not come back empty-handed. They'll do the work I sent them to do, they'll complete the assignment I gave them."

I am a very different person today than I was five years ago. I was immature, impatient, selfish, and angry. I also had unrealistic ideas about marriage, relationships, and life expectations. If it was up to me, I would've gotten married in 2010, but I may not have been able to handle the responsibility of marriage or showing my husband unconditional love. I wouldn't be able to manage my emotions and seek God when I needed guidance.

During those five years, I explored and strengthen my relationship with Christ. I attended a singles ministry called Singles Pleasing the Lord, joined a women's accountability group, traveled to various conferences, increased my faith in God, and figured out my purpose and spiritual gifts. I confronted issues that I had repressed such as disappointment and rejection which I had experienced in my youth. Sometimes we don't realize how previous experiences shape our current perspective. If I had gotten out the lane of development God placed me in, I would've missed opportunities to enhance my mind, body, and soul. I would've been sabotaging the future I hoped for because I was impatient and couldn't see the bigger picture.

I was married for about a year before I separated from my husband and filed for a divorce a year later. It was very difficult time for me because I spent a lot of time regretting decisions I had made. There were red flags that I overlooked and I let myself get so involved in his life & aspirations that I started to neglect my own desires and dreams. During the divorce process I joined a support group at my church called DivorceCare. The group provided me with a safe place to express my feelings, learn how to cope with the loss, and helped me understand that God still loves me despite my divorce. This was one of the biggest traffic jams I experienced in my life. The rollercoaster of emotions I felt ranged from sadness to anger, and disappointment to relief. It took some time but I've taken steps to help in my healing process. It's taken me almost 30 years to realize that I can't control time. It's about time!

It's very easy to look at your watch, clock, or calendar and think that your timing is off. There is a saying that if life gives you lemons make lemonade. Well if life gives you lemons take them to the Lord and let Him turn them into new wine. He can take situations that seem like mistakes or setbacks and cause them to be your motivation which inspires others to seek His face. It's all about perspective. A "wrong turn" may seem like it has the potential to ruin your plans but, if you have a relationship with the Lord and know that He loves you, that God wants what's best for you, and He is faithful towards you, and forgives you. Your steps are ordered by the Lord.

Words for the Road

The clock on the dashboard can only tell you the time not the season.

6
TIME WILL TELL

Although I don't know what the future holds, God has a plan for us. Jeremiah 29:11 (MSG) says "I know what I'm doing. I have it all planned out - plans to take care of you, not to abandon you, plans to give you the future you hope for." Who knows what circumstances and obstacles will come their way? Who cares? Everyone, but God told us not to worry. As I increase my faith in God's ability to provide for me and fulfill his plan for my life, I am at peace. This is a process that takes time. If you are having a hard time with how your life is progressing, meditate on Matthew 6:27-34 MSG:

[27-29] "Has anyone, by fussing in front of the mirror ever gotten taller by so much as an inch? All this time and money wasted on fashion—do you think it makes that much difference? Instead of looking at the fashions, walk out into the fields and look at the wildflowers. They never primp or shop, but have you ever seen color and design quite like it? The ten best-dressed men and women in the country look shabby alongside them.

[30-33] "If God gives such attention to the appearance of wildflowers—most of which are never even seen—don't you think he'll attend to you, take pride in you, do his best for you? What I'm trying to do here is to get you to relax, to not be so preoccupied with *getting*, so you can respond to God's *giving*. People who don't know God and the way he works fuss over these things, but you

know both God and how he works. Steep your life in God-reality, God-initiative, God-provisions. Don't worry about missing out. You'll find all your everyday human concerns will be met.[34] "Give your entire attention to what God is doing right now, and don't get worked up about what may or may not happen tomorrow. God will help you deal with whatever hard things come up when the time comes."

Stop worrying about traffic jams. Focus on what God is teaching you while you are in traffic jams. You may have experienced your own lessons learned from traffic jams. Share them with others. Our testimonies are tools to help others deal with similar situations. Although you might not be ready to do so immediately, let the Lord lead and guide you. We are in traffic jams, traffic jams are not us.

Words for the Road

Don't let a traffic jam change who you are or where you are going.

WORDS FOR THE ROAD

- Detours may be a part of your destiny.

- Don't worry about being passed up by others they may not be going to the same place you are.

- If the light is yellow, don't rush to get past it; wait patiently while it's red.

- You may be stuck behind a slow car for a reason; you might not know the reason now or later.

- Your speed is relative to the road you are on; it is different on side streets, in alleys, in a school or construction zone, and on expressways.

- Yelling at other drivers is unnecessary they can't even hear you.

- Don't call people names unless it's how God sees them; use words like Beautiful, Blessed, Anointed, Apple (of His eye) and Son or Daughter.

- Don't rush to your destination. There might not be a parking spot for you once you get there.

- If there is a train in front of you, just be still; taking a detour will waste your gas and energy.

- Getting lost can be frustrating but you are never lost if God is with you.

- When a passenger is along for the ride, don't let them be your primary guide.

- U-turns are permitted in life; it's never too late to change your course.

- Pit stops are necessary but don't let a pit stop become your destination.

- Allow God to be your compass.

- More than one route will get you where you're going; just make sure God is your GPS.

- Whether you have experienced a fender binder (minor), a head on collision, roll over (major) or other types of traumatic incidents, He will give you peace.

- You get a car wash and oil change frequently. Do the same maintenance on your body, mind, and soul.

- As a driver or rider, we may not realize that pedestrians are watching our every move.

- Larger vehicles have a harder time stopping; if you have been struggling with something for a long time it may take you longer to stop.

- If you have a wide load or lots of cargo, (hurts, disappointments, tragedies, collisions, and infractions) it may take God a longer time to heal and deliver you.

IT'S BEEN TOO LONG! LESSONS LEARNED FROM TRAFFIC JAMS

- Slower vehicles prevent accidents, navigate detours, and recover easily.

- The timing for a construction project varies on several factors including the maturity of the work crew, investment in the project, and traffic patterns.

- Remember, no matter which road you take the Lord will make you successful.

- Your journey is about you and God, so know Him for yourself.

- People can look at you crazy while you are in a traffic jam but it's between you and God.

- When you reach road blocks, red lights, U-turns, or changing road conditions, know that He is still in control.

- Let Him be the center of your joy in the midst traffic jams.

- Changing your speed may cause you to bypass God's blessings and plan for your life.

- It's okay to let someone in front of you in traffic because you will get there when He is ready for you to.

- Pray for those who are rushing to their destination.

- You are not the only person who is stuck in a traffic jam; someone else is experiencing the same thing you are.

- Don't always ride alone, car pool occasionally to get motivation from others; let God choose your companion.

- Don't let where you are now affect where you are going later.

- If you let where you want to go be your inspiration, where you are now won't be an issue.

- A detour is a slight/considerable change in route due to hazards, construction, or timing to reach a destination; although this may increase the length of your drive, you should still reach your destination.

QUESTIONS FOR YOUR JOURNEY

What is your purpose?

What is your passion? What are your gifts?

Who or what inspires you to stay on the road of life?

_____
_____
_____
_____
_____
_____
_____
_____
_____

How do you deal with your personal traffic jams?

_____
_____
_____
_____
_____
_____
_____
_____
_____

IT'S BEEN TOO LONG! LESSONS LEARNED FROM TRAFFIC JAMS

Where is your spiritual gas tank, on Empty, ¼ Tank, ½ Tank, ¾ Tank, or Full? What ways can you increase your spiritual fuel?

_____
_____
_____
_____
_____
_____
_____
_____
_____

Where is your spiritual gas station? Which ministries and organizations help sustain your energy?

_____
_____
_____
_____
_____
_____
_____
_____
_____

Who is part of your support system when you are in traffic jams?

_____
_____
_____
_____
_____
_____
_____
_____
_____

Which scriptures help you during traffic jams?

_____
_____
_____
_____
_____
_____
_____
_____
_____

PRAYER FOR TRAFFIC JAMS

Dear Lord,

We thank you for the lessons that you have taught us in the middle of traffic jams. Help us deal with life's circumstances which try to disrupt our relationships, attitudes, and perspective on life. We ask that you give us peace and patience no matter what mode of transportation we use. Continually remind us that we are blessed to be in the land of the living and that no situation can change the plans you have for us. Detours are not our destination. You said in your Word that your plans are to prospers us and not harm us Father. Let us show kindness to our neighbors, coworkers, strangers, and everyone we come in contact with. If we are not morning people keep us from disrupting other people's day with our attitude. Help us plant seeds of positivity in our communities and around the world. Lord if there is someone who doesn't know you personally speak to their heart. Show them how you have brought them through trials and allowed them to stay on course. In Jesus name we pray.

Amen

HELPFUL RESOURCES

WEBSITES

- Singles Pleasing The Lord

    www.singlespleasingthelord.com

- Spiritual Gift Test

    http://www.spiritualgiftstest.com/

- The 5 Love Languages

    http://www.5lovelanguages.com/

- Discovery Your God Given Purpose

    https://www.focusonthefamily.com/faith/faith-in-life/discovering-your-god-given-purpose/discovering-your-god-given-purpose

- Divorce Care

    https://www.divorcecare.org

BOOKS

- *The 5 Love Languages* – Gary D. Chapman

- *Things I Wish I'd Known Before We got Married* – Gary D. Chapman

- *How to Get Past Disappointment (Matters of the Heart Series)* - Michelle McKinney Hammond

- *What to Do Until Love Finds You: The Bestselling Guide to Preparing Yourself for Your Perfect Mate* - Michelle McKinney Hammond

- Before You Say "I Do" –H. Norman Wright and Wes Roberts

MUSIC
ALBUMS

Erica Campbell – *Help*

Tasha Cobbs – *Grace*

Travis Greene – *The Hill*

William McDowell – *Arise*

Jonathan McReynolds – *Life Music*

Jonathan McReynolds - *Life Music: Stage Two*

William Murphy – *God Chaser*

Marvin Sapp - *Here I Am*

SONGS

Alexis Spight – Don't Worry

Brian Courtney Wilson – "Worth Fighting For"

Donald Lawrence & The Tri –City Singers – "Encourage Yourself"

GEI & Kierra Sheard – Hang On

Jekalyn Carr – "Greater is Coming"

James Fortune & FIYA – "I Believe"

Jessica Reedy – Better

Jessica Reedy – Put It On The Altar

Kirk Franklin – "My Life Is In Your Hands"

Marvin Sapp – "My Testimony"

Mary Mary – "Can't Give Up Now"

Pastor Hezekiah Walker – Moving Forward

Tasha Cobbs- Fill Me Up

Travis Greene- Intentional

Travis Greene- Thank You For Being God

William Murphy – Already Getting Better

Yolanda Adams – "I'm Gonna Be Ready"

ABOUT THE AUTHOR

DarLisa L. Meaders was born and raised on the South Side of Chicago, IL. She has overcome many traffic jams in life and is passionate about helping others accomplish their goals. In 2010, she graduated from Grand Valley State University with a Bachelor's Degree in Biomedical Science. Her elective courses during college sparked her interest in the Public Health field. She became more passionate about preventing disease and promoting healthy lifestyles through health education. After a year of service with AmeriCorps she attended University of Illinois at Chicago School of Public Health Master's Program.

Over the next few years she graduated with her Master's in Public Health but couldn't find a full-time position in the field. She became irritated, frustrated, and discouraged with her circumstances; however, she realized that she wasn't the only experiencing traffic jams. There are many people young and old who have felt discouraged at some point in their life. She took a stand and declared that where she is right now won't be where she'll be forever.

After surviving one of the biggest traffic jams of her life she vowed to thrive and redefined herself as a Destined Determined Dreamer (D3). She is on a mission to help others realize the triumphs in the midst of their trials through public speaking, inspirational apparel, and publishing books.

DarLisa likes to make people laugh, eat, ride horses, spend time with her family and friends, and try new things. If you would like to hear DarLisa speak at a church, school, conference, or any other event, she can be reached at d3ndlm@gmail.com. Feel free to provide any questions or feedback to this email. The author is working on the second book in the It's Been Too Long Series called Don't Lose Momentum. She thanks you for your support.

www.ingramcontent.com/pod-product-compliance
Lightning Source LLC
Chambersburg PA
CBHW041308110426
42743CB00037B/35